Birdhouse Beauties
Jewelry Decorated Homes for Birds and Bird Lovers

Hillside House Publishing
2015

Birdhouse Beauties: Jewelry Decorated Homes for Birds and Bird Lovers

Copyright © 2015 by Holly DiBella-McCarthy

All rights reserved. This book or any portion thereof
may not be reproduced or used in any manner whatsoever
without the express written permission of the publisher
except for the use of brief quotations in a review.

Hillside House Publishing

P.O. Box 391, Venice, FL 34284

Contact:

birdhousebeautiesbyholly@gmail.com

Birdhouse Beauties P.O. Box 246 Tolland, CT 06084

Credits:

Book Cover Design: Joe McCarthy, Sandbox Arts, LLC neckahneck@gmail.com

Book layout: Author, Joe McCarthy

Book Photo Editor: Joe McCarthy

Book Editors: Jan Mann, Karen Hoke, Michele Colletti

Photographs: Author, with the exception of pages 12, 13, 16, 17, 18, 20, 22, 24 (c), 28 Joe McCarthy; and page 42 (b) and cover (d) Harold A. Mann

ISBN 978-0-9777174-4-6

Printed in the United States of America

Dedicated to:

Kevin Joseph McCarthy, my soul-mate and best friend. I love you more!

Special thanks to:

My flock: Joseph, for following your passion and inspiring me to do the same; Brendan, for reminding me through your example to never quit until the job is done; Mikayla, for your positive outlook and comparing me to Curious George; my sisters: Karen Hoke, for urging me to write this book and your consistent enthusiasm; Michele Colletti, for the book title and your infectious energy; my parents: Michael J. DiBella Jr., who takes pride in my every accomplishment, and Jan Mann, a fellow author whose never ending support and encouragement exemplifies "a mother's love."

In Memory of:

Grampy Mann, who shared his love of photography and nature, and who taught me that patience leads to success.

Contents

Introduction	8

Answers to Your Questions

Why This Book?	11
How Do I Choose the Right Birdhouse to Decorate?	12
What Supplies Will I Need?	18
Where Can I Find the Jewelry?	19

Imagining, Creating, and Finishing a Birdhouse

Preparing the House	20
Painting the House	22
Decorating with Jewelry	26
Finishing Touches	31

Displaying and Viewing Your Masterpiece

Decorative and Useful Indoor Treasures	32
Mounting Your Outdoor Masterpiece	35
Final Thoughts	43

Charts

Birdhouse Size Recommendations	15
Nesting Home Placement	40

Introduction

My craving to create was born in a college photography class, where I learned that viewing life through the lens of a camera provides an opportunity to discover treasures hidden in plain sight. Over the years, I have found that the process of making art, whether it is taking pictures, writing, and even home decorating, has the power to open new worlds.

Creating, beginning with an original idea and ending with a distinct product, rejuvenates both mind and soul. Too often, I find myself with only enough time to dream about the art I might make. I have written complete novels and finished beautiful art pieces — in my head — and once I fill the final page or add the last bit of detail, the vision slowly fades to oblivion.

I admire the working artists amongst us. Full time artists have the luxury of time — time to contemplate and expand ideas, and then follow their passion through to a finished work of art. But I also think there are many people just like me who have chosen a different path for their life's work, yet still long for a creative outlet.

This book is for those who search for inspiration, and once discovered, benefit by a step-by-step manual that guides them to project completion.

I can't pinpoint exactly how the idea of jewelry-embellished birdhouses developed. Perhaps while driving, or walking my dog, or maybe it was in a meditative shower. Was it when I was trying to untangle old jewelry discovered in a long forgotten box? I only know that when I stood in front of a row of unfinished birdhouses in the craft store, and thought of all the jewelry I was no longer wearing, yet couldn't bear to part with, the image became clear.

Obsessively, I planned every detail of my initial design. Because I decorated the first birdhouse with jewelry from my own past, memories re-surfaced with each carefully placed piece. My first prom, honeymoon pearls, a beach vacation, holidays with family, yard sales with friends. And when the little house was completed, I knew I had fashioned something special.

As my interest in all things "bird" grew, ideas for birdhouses crafted for indoor decoration soon expanded to outdoor creations. I read everything I could about birds, nesting preferences, and birdhouses. I watched the bird activity around my house during the frigid northeast winter, and throughout the spring and summer months. In the process, I reconnected with my long-held curiosity with the fascinating life of birds.

My love of birds, merged with other lifelong interests — crafting, photography, and writing — inspired these designs. The possibilities for unique bird homes are truly endless. So, while juggling all of life's responsibilities and passions — go ahead! Create in your mind's eye! And, when the how-to steps become clear, your visions will lead to beautiful, one-of-a-kind creations.

My first birdhouse? It's on the first page of this book, displayed with a stuffed canary in memory of my childhood pet, Chirpy.

Answers to Your Questions

Why This Book?

This book is for you because **you**

- enjoy crafts
- feel creative at the moment
- have a stash of broken, unwanted, but cherished jewelry
- need an excuse to go to a yard or estate sale
- love the idea of creating a unique treasure you can display today
- like birds and want to learn more about them
- want to embrace the challenge of making a nesting home birds will use
- look to beautify your home outdoors or inside, or
- long to create a WOW gift for someone special.

How Do I Choose the Right Birdhouse to Decorate?

The birdhouse you decorate will be influenced by where you want to display it. First, decide if you want to create a functional outdoor home, or an inside decoration. Next, match size and shape with your chosen location and finally, consider birdhouse style. Knowing the ultimate displaying spot will help you choose a compatible house.

If you want to hang your finished birdhouse outdoors, will it be mounted in your garden or on your house? Perhaps it will be hanging on a tree or in your gazebo. Maybe you want to secure it to a fence or a post. Consider a place that will allow for maximum viewing pleasure from a window, porch, or yard. Nesting homes are specially constructed to protect bird families from a variety of weather conditions.

You can also choose to bring a sense of nature indoors where a decorated birdhouse (and perhaps a fake feathered friend) will become a conversation piece in a gathering place in your home.

Indoor birdhouses are typically made from lightweight wood. Made for decorating, these homes are available in countless styles from large Victorian mansions to cozy and quaint cottages. These are simply too fragile to display outdoors. The weather would destroy their vivid colors and intricate designs, and even worse loosen the glue that holds them together. They are not for the wild birds but they are for bird lovers!

Home Features

If you decide to construct a birdhouse yourself, there are plenty of excellent references available to guide you. This book is not one of them. I tried to like the idea of finding a blueprint, gathering the saws, drill, hammer, screwdriver, nails, and other assorted tools, but I was too excited to start decorating!

If you want to create a birdhouse for a decoration, any size, shape, hole dimension, and mounting option will work fine. Place the unfinished house in the spot where it will be displayed, then stand back and imagine it painted and embellished with jewelry; if it looks great, you have selected the right style.

When decorating an outside nesting home, determine which bird species you hope to attract. Whether you make your own or, like me, buy fully constructed unfinished birdhouses my **Birdhouse Size Recommendations** chart will help you make the right choice to attract the birds you want to see. The specified sizes are approximate and should be used as a general guide. Most birds are not particularly fussy about their living quarters, so don't be surprised if you follow the dimensions for a Tree Swallow, but a Bluebird moves in!

One day after this house was mounted, a Chickadee moved in. Two months later, and a few ounces heavier, this songbird began having difficulty fitting through the hole. Not to be deterred, home renovations began!

Cardinals will not be moving into a decorated house, as these beauties prefer to build nests in dense shrubbery. Have plenty of cracked corn and sunflower seed-filled feeders nearby, and Cardinals will find you!

Birdhouse Size Recommendations

Species	Birdhouse Height in inches	Floor Dimensions in inches	Entry-Hole Size in inches	Hole Height Above Floor in inches
Bluebirds Eastern, Western, and Mountain	8-10	5 x 5	1 ½	6
Chickadees Black-capped, Chestnut-backed, and Mountain	8-12	4 x 4	1 1/8 -1 ½	6-8
Finch House and Purple	5-7	6 x 6	1 3/8 - 2	4-6
Flicker Northern	16+	7 x 7	2 ¾	12+
Flycatchers Many varieties	9 - 12	6 x 6	1 ½-2 ½	6 - 8
Kestral American	14 -16	8 x 8	3	10 - 12
Martin Purple	6	6 x 6	2 - 2 ½	1 - 1 ¾
Nuthatches Red Breasted, White Breasted	8 - 12	4 x 4	1 1/8 -1 ½	6 - 8
Owl Barn Screech Barred Saw-whet	15 - 18 12 - 18 16 15 - 18	10 x 18 8 x 8 14 x 14 8 x 8	6 - 8 3 - 4 6 - 8 3 - 4	4 9 - 12 14 - 18 10 - 12
Robin American and English	8	6 x 6	No hole, open-sided with roof	—
Sparrow House	9 - 12	4 x 4	1 ½ - 2	6 - 8
Swallow Tree	6 - 12	5 x 5	1 ¼ - 1 ½	3 - 6
Titmice Plain, Tufted, and Bridled	8 - 12	4 x 4	1 ¼ - 1 ½	6 - 8
Warbler Prothonary	8 - 12	4 x 4	1 ¼ - 1 ½	5 - 7
Wood Duck	14+	6 x 6	3 x 4 (oval)	12 - 16
Wrens House, Bewicks, Carolina	8 x 12	8 x 12	1 - 1 ¼ 1 ¼ - 1 ½	4 - 6

Buying Your Birdhouse

Online stores offer plenty of possibilities. If the site you choose does not provide dimensions, ask before you type in your credit card information. Ebay may work for you. I found an unused vintage birdhouse made in the 70s for $5.99. Look in craft stores with coupons in hand — I have purchased many fine homes for half price! Search yard and estate sales. You may find a house already painted and you can decide to use it as is or to repaint it. Hardware stores, unfinished furniture stores, and lawn and garden shops are other possibilities. Knowing if you are creating a birdhouse for a decorated keepsake or to attract live nesting birds will help direct your search.

Unlike decorative homes, outdoor birdhouses are constructed with thicker wood. Wood that is ½ to ¾ inch thick ensures protection of the birds from excessive heat or cold. A roof overhang of at least one inch will also protect them from sun, rain, or snow. A removable feature will allow the home to be opened and cleaned for new residents the next year. You will also be able to provide inside accents such as grooves or wire mesh to help the baby birds climb up for their launch! Proper ventilation is equally important, so look for extra holes or slits at the top or the sides. Make sure there is a drainage hole or slat on the bottom so water will not accumulate.

And now for a myth-breaker . . . a perch is not needed on a birdhouse! Cavity nesting birds do not need a perch to enter a birdhouse or feed their young. Now, perches are pretty and it's not a bad thing if you want to keep yours, but perches may also be an invitation for unwanted company. I sometimes keep the perch on and other times remove it, because in either case if you have all the other features listed, a bird will occupy the residence.

The unfinished birdhouse you buy will not be perfect. The wood may be rough in spots. There may be visible nicks or splits in the wood, or the pieces may not fit together snugly. It will undoubtedly have visible nail holes. The house you choose may have added features you don't care for like the perch, or lack features you want such as a predator guard placed around the entrance hole (block of wood with a same sized hole cut.) Any of these imperfections are okay. Smile and be glad you found a house with the size and specs for the type of bird you want to attract. You will soon learn how to mask the flaws and prepare your birdhouse as a comfortable and attractive nesting home.

What Supplies Will I Need?

Preparation:	wood putty, sand paper
Paint and finishing:	acrylic paint, finishing spray
Glue choices:	a superglue, epoxy, or craft glue
Tools:	scissors, wire clippers, needle-nosed pliers, Phillips screwdriver, metal file, small handsaw and/or drill
Mounting supplies:	chain or rope and screws, wood strip with drilled hole, or a flange and mounting pole
Add-ons to consider:	wire mesh, hole protectors, wood shavings, and of course, the jewelry!

Glue Choices

To attach plastic, glass, metal, and ceramic jewelry to outdoor birdhouses, a superglue sets in 30-60 seconds on wood. This type is especially useful when securing uneven jewelry backs on rough wood. Epoxy also adheres to a variety of materials and sets in 10-20 minutes which allows time for repositioning of jewelry. Once dry, both a superglue and epoxy are waterproof and are largely unaffected by extreme hot or cold temperatures. Craft or "tacky glue" should only be used for indoor decorations, but if the birdhouse will be exposed to moisture it is best to use a superglue or epoxy. Craft glues can take 4-6 hours to dry, so you should only glue jewelry onto one side of the house at a time.

Where Can I Find the Jewelry?

The best place to find jewelry is in your own drawer. What women collect over the years can amass to a decorated birdhouse masterpiece! Pendants, broaches, pins, bracelets, and earrings are all potential birdhouse embellishments. Another option is to ask family members and friends if they have old or outdated jewelry they want to donate. I called my sister immediately after opening the bag of jewelry she gave me. I was overwhelmed at the sheer quantity thrown into the plastic bag as well as the beauty and quality of some of the pieces.

She just laughed and told me "this is stuff that's been hanging around for years that I won't ever wear, but was just too beautiful to toss." One woman's trash is another woman's treasure . . . Yard and estate sales often sell jewelry which the owners no longer want. I have found authentic vintage (my favorite to decorate with) as well as distinctive handmade signed pieces, magnificent mosaic, and exquisite sterling silver on tables in yards and garages, and at flea markets, fairs, and church bazaars.

Imagining, Creating, and Finishing a Birdhouse Beauty

Preparing the House

Take a good look at the house you purchased to assess if all the features that are needed exist. For decorative indoor bird houses, you may want to add detail such as roof shingles, a chimney, or a sweet little fence.

You can also create functional indoor houses. Choose to make a planter, tissue box holder, or jewelry keeper. By removing the roof and sanding the edges, you can design a useful decoration for your home or a bird loving friend.

For outdoor birdhouses that you plan to use to attract nesting birds, determine if the house has the necessary extras listed in **Buying your Birdhouse** on page 16. If venting slats or bottom drainage holes are not present, use a saw or drill to add them. If your house does not have a clean-out function such as a screwed in bottom or swing out door, you will also want to construct one of these. My favorite idea for adding this feature came with my vintage birdhouse find. On the back, the builder added a cute oval door with a hinge on one side and a latch on the other. Clever!

Now it's time to cover all unwanted nail holes, cracks, or indentations with wood putty. Allow putty to dry completely, usually in 1-6 hours depending on the depth of the hole being filled. I mostly use latex wood filler and sometimes a spackling paste. Directions for use will be listed on the specific product you choose. In general, start with a dry, clean surface. Overfill slightly the spot being filled and allow to dry thoroughly before sanding.

Next, use sandpaper to smooth the entire house. I use fine grit sandpaper on the filled areas and medium on rougher areas such as roof edges. Once finished sanding, be sure to wipe away all waste completely. Now your house is ready for painting.

Painting the House

For **decorative indoor birdhouses** — Painting your house a dark color such as black or navy will showcase all colors of jewelry beautifully, and will result in a rich and classy look. Painting the roof silver or gold, depending on the color jewelry, will add to the elegance. A brightly painted-house may be the "pop" your room needs in an otherwise nondescript corner. You may choose to paint your decoration the same color as the room wall, which is another great way to highlight the jewels. Using painter's tape to create color blocks will result in a modern look when bright colors are used, and a vintage look when pastels are used. Once you know where the house will be displayed, your paint choices will become apparent.

For **functional outdoor birdhouses** — Paint and stain should not contain lead or creosote. If your unfinished house has interesting wood grain, you may choose to use linseed oil to keep a more natural look. If you use this, wait several days for the oil to dry completely before decorating. For outdoor birdhouses, **never** paint the inside of the house or the inside of the entrance hole. High gloss paints and finishing sealants should not be used. Instead, choose products with a matte finish. If the house will be mounted primarily in the sun use light colors. Darker colors absorb more heat and may keep the house too warm for the birds. Purple Martin houses should always be painted white. When decorating an outdoor birdhouse, keep in mind that very bright colors may deter some birds from moving in. On the other hand, remember, most birds are not fussy. When they are ready to nest, any empty home will be considered!

Use 2 or 3 coats of acrylic paint for a rich look. Professional heavy body acrylic works well on roofs and rough wood. Paint the light colors first so the darker shades can cover small mistakes.

Experiment with color. I ultimately decided on the bright red roof atop this bold orange house.

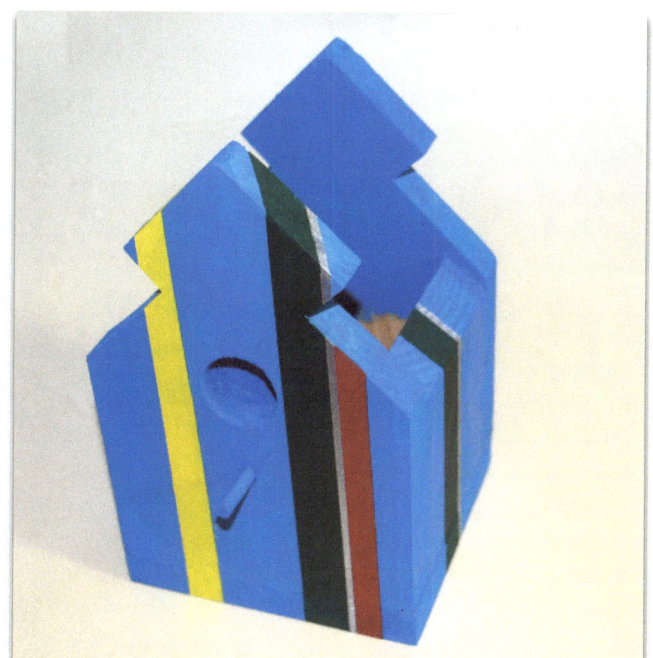

Vertical stripes of various colors and widths created with painter's tape are perfect on this functional indoor planter. To begin, the roof was removed and edges were sanded. A piece of wood was Super-glued over the inside of the entrance hole. The house was painted inside and out with a bright blue acrylic. Stripes were added, jewelry glued, and finishing spray was applied. A plastic container holding succulents was placed inside and the plants became the new roof!

Have fun designing rooftops!

Linseed oil, painted tree branches with leaves, and an added predator guard prepare this house to blend in to a woodsy backdrop. If you choose to use a water-based stain, a large soft brush works best on rough wood. You can also leave the raw wood as is and watch nature determine new color shades.

This church needed a door! Painter's tape allowed for clean lines.

Decorating With Jewelry

Start by laying jewelry pieces on your chosen house. Move pieces around and enjoy experimenting with different arrangements. Keep an eye out for that small part, such as one charm from a bracelet or portion of an earring, that when separated from the original piece will make a big statement on your house. It may take some time to determine what combination of jewelry works best for the style of house and display area you have chosen. But, this is part of the creative process and part of the fun!

Gather tools, including needle-nose pliers, wire cutters, scissors, and metal file, along with the collection of jewelry you are considering. As each bit of jewelry is unique, there is no one right way to prepare a piece for gluing. First, examine the piece you want to prepare. Next, do what you can to ensure it will lay as flat as possible on the part of the birdhouse you choose to glue it on. The metal bits of jewelry are normally quite pliable and parts can usually be bent or filed down with a metal file.

Pins and brooches typically have flat backs, which make them perfect for a snug fit on the flat sides of a birdhouse. Most pins on modern brooches are glued and can be removed by using pliers in a curling-twisting motion. Pins attached to vintage brooches were often welded directly on multiple layers of the brooch. If this is the case, cut each side of the pin part off and then use pliers to push remaining raised edges to lay flat. Should you decide to use pliers to remove the pin and the brooch parts separate, you can glue the separate layers back together.

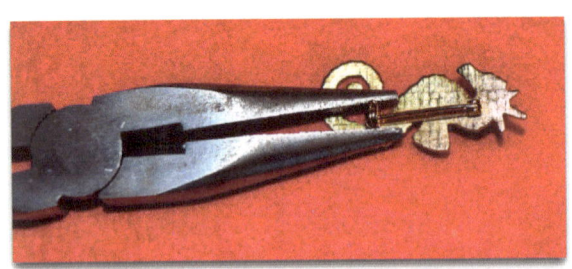

Many earring posts can be removed with pliers by bending the post side-to-side. If you choose to cut the post down with a wire cutter, the end that is left can be pushed into most wood. Along with the glue, this method will provide extra security. Earring wires may be cut off with wire cutters and remaining rough ends can be filed away with a metal file.

Necklace or bracelet chain parts can also be cut with a wire cutter. Scissors are often strong enough to cut plastic or thin wire between the stones, beads, or links. After the cut is made, tape the ends to keep beads from sliding off if you plan to glue a large section on the house. Clasps, bails, or O-rings can be cut off and filed smooth.

If you plan to cover all surfaces on a house or roof, cut a piece of paper the same size as the wood you plan to cover. Position jewelry on this to allow for multiple design variations until the perfect arrangement appears. Before gluing, angle the house so the pitch of the roof or side of the house is level. Allow to dry completely before repeating on the next side.

A few carefully placed pieces can be the beginning of a story that needs to be told.

Moonlit Magic

Finishing Touches

Let your decorated birdhouse dry for 24 hours. The final step is to seal and protect the house. If the birdhouse will be used for nesting, cover the birdhouse hole and any vent slats and drain holes with painter's tape. Birds will often peck at these entrance holes and you want to protect them from harmful chemicals. I use a Polyurethane spray that is fast drying, non-yellowing and UV resistant. Spray your birdhouse in a well-ventilated area, preferably outdoors. The temperature should be between 50 and 90 degrees and humidity should be low. Set the birdhouse at eye level on a tarp or in a cardboard box. This will trap the excess, so yard flowers and your car will be safe from the sealant! After shaking the can well, spray using a back and forth motion 10 to 15 inches from the house. This next part is important — coat the surface lightly because if the coating is too thick there will be visible drips. Allow the sprayed surface to dry, then turn the house and repeat. A second coat can be sprayed, especially if the house will be subjected to extreme weather. Following the final coat of sealer, allow your birdhouse to dry for 24 hours before mounting.

Displaying and Viewing Your Masterpiece

Decorative and Useful Indoor Treasures

Birdhouses created for an inside decoration can be displayed in just about any room in your home! Use a color paint to compliment your existing color scheme, or use a contrasting color to display as a room focal point. Perch one high on an upper kitchen cabinet, or arrange several houses in a row 6-8 inches apart to avoid a crowded look. Settle one on a hutch in the dining room with a nest and a few feathered friends, or low on a windowsill among your plants. Set one on a fireplace mantel, or a bookshelf in your home. Several birdhouses can even be hung on a bare wall in a vertical arrangement for an instant conversation starter! Use one as a table centerpiece and accent with acorns and twigs from outside. Decorate houses with seasonal jewelry for a sweet holiday party centerpiece. Use these creative ideas for displaying decorative birdhouses indoors, and set up a gorgeous display that will add color and unique style to your home.

Decorated birdhouses can also be fashioned to serve a useful purpose. Roofs can be removed to allow a variety of home items to nest with panache! Store a tissue box, cotton balls, make-up brushes, and other vanity necessities in one. Recipe cards can rest in a box on a kitchen counter. Place one on your desk for letters received. Plasticware placed in a decorated house and set on a picnic table doubles as a seasonal centerpiece. Decorate several to hold indoor plants. A jewelry holder can be made with roof on or off by gluing the jewels to extend beyond the box edges to allow necklaces, bracelets, and rings to hang. Look in each room of your home and discover that the possibilities for serviceable decorations are endless!

Before

After

Use profession themed jewelry. Teachers receive lots of trinkets! Create a "starter house" for a favorite teacher and gift with a note suggesting she add some of her own collection.

Compliment room colors and style. Add jewelry that makes you happy!

Functional is fun! Expand the perch, and add leaves and keys to create a cute jewelry holder.

You may decide your decorative birdhouse belongs outside. If you followed the directions in the **Finishing Touches** section on page 31, and keep it away from wet weather, it can be enjoyed for years hanging from a covered deck or gazebo. You may find as I did, when you least expect it, that what you once made for decoration has been taken over by birds!

Your house will also do fine in a 3 or 4 season sunroom or porch. These spaces are intended for reflection and relaxation. Decorating a house with jewelry from your personal collection will conjure up memories. Choosing jewelry that says something about who you are will invite conversation.

Company waiting!

Mounting Your Outdoor Masterpiece

Placement Choices

Mounting your outdoor birdhouse will require some planning and thought. Before choosing a specific spot consider visibility, direction, habitat, height, stability, and species preference. I often start by standing in various viewing locations. From my front windows and porch I can see shrubs, various trees such as maple, evergreen, and apple, and a fence along the driveway. My back deck faces a wooded area with larger trees. The most important question for me is — will I be able to enjoy watching birds using the birdhouse?

You must also consider direction when choosing a location. In general, a birdhouse should face east or south, although some of the smaller nesting birds are not as particular and will nest in a house facing any direction.

Traditionally, birdhouses are mounted in trees and you will need to spend some time choosing the perfect branch that will provide safety, stability, and a good viewing angle. A nail or screw can be used to secure the house to the tree. Remember to leave some space to loosen the screw each year to allow for healthy tree growth. Mounting a birdhouse near shrubbery will allow a bird's confidence to grow as most like to survey for safety before entering. Mounting directly onto your house is also a possibility if you want to attract birds such as wrens, which are more tolerant of the human species. You can also mount on a fence; however, if the fence is used near livestock, the birdhouse should face away from the animals.

Another possibility is the use of a mounting pole where the birdhouse is attached and a specific height can be realized. The poles protect from predators as they can be mounted high and are difficult to climb. A 6 foot long, ½ to 1-inch threaded galvanized pipe works well. A pipe cap placed over the threads before pounding into the ground will protect the threads from damage. Drive the pole about a foot deep or until sturdy. Attach a floor flange with galvanized screws to the bottom of the house, remove the pipe cap and screw the house on. Use of a flange allows you to rotate the birdhouse to face the optimal direction for the tenant you hope to attract. Best of all, just unscrew the house to easily manage your landlord maintenance and repair obligations!

Consider Habitat

When you selected your house you may have chosen the dimensions and hole size to attract a certain species of bird. Now it's important to consider the best habitat to mount your creation for the birds you want to attract. For example, the Robin's nesting shelf can be secured to a tree in your yard or woods edge, or even placed under the eaves of your house, garage, or outbuildings. Don't be surprised to find that the Robin missed a great home ownership opportunity when Doves move into the box first, as the two species shop for the same style house!

The Finch's house can be closer to your doorstep as these birds typically stay close to humans. If you have ever had a bird build a nest in one of your hanging plants, it was most likely a finch! Go ahead and try hanging your birdhouse right on your porch or wedge it inside a hanging plant where the flowers and foliage will act as a barrier to the hot sun. There is a plethora of bird books containing mounds of information on bird habitat. For your purposes, it may be enough to know the basics in the **Nesting Home Placement** chart on page 40.

Your birdhouse can be mounted in any season. Many species such as Chickadees are year-round residents and will discover the birdhouse makes a fine roosting spot during the nighttime. It is in the late winter or early spring that most species will choose their nesting spot. Although I have mounted in the winter months (to be sure the birdhouses created will withstand harsh winters, drenching rain, and terrific winds), I prefer to hang 2-3 weeks before early spring. In general, southerners should place birdhouses by February, and for those living in northern regions, by mid to late March. Once I hang a birdhouse, it remains in its chosen spot for many years. I do open the homes to empty the remnants in late fall, but then reattach in hopes future generations of the same bird family will occupy the home the following spring.

Hang in late winter.

Birds shop in early spring.

By summer, families are well protected.

Other Comforts of Home

Another task you can do to convince birds to use the mounted house is to provide nesting materials nearby. Take a suet holder or even an empty string bag like the ones used to hold onions, and stuff it with materials birds can use to build their nest. Materials can include string, feathers, hair, dryer lint, and/or small pieces of burlap or material. Hang the filled holder from a tree branch or pole close to the house. Certain species appreciate 1-2 inches of non-scented wood shavings or saw dust in the bottom of the birdhouse. These birds include Chickadees, Flickers, Nuthatches, and Wood Ducks. Birds need water near their homes, so mount your birdhouse close to a natural water source if possible, or place a birdbath or small bowl in an open area nearby. If you create a small water pool on the ground and keep the area wet, mud will form. Barn Swallows and Robins will use the mud to build their nest. Bird feeders placed in an open area will also be attractive to birds searching for just the right real estate!

I mounted this Humming bird nesting house too close to the feeder. Next spring, I will move the feeder at least 10 feet away from the house. I will leave the nesting materials close by.

Nesting Home Placement

Bluebird
Mount in open lawn or field, or lawn with scattered trees and low or scant ground cover; Mountain and Western Bluebirds will also use forest edges. Entrance hole should face an open area. Bluebirds prefer east, north, and south facing directions.
Box Height: 3-6 feet

Purple Martin
Mount on pole in expansive open area in meadows, fields, farmland, swamps, ponds, lakes, or rivers with unobstructed space for scavenging flying insects. There should be no trees or structures within 40 feet of the Martin pole in any direction.
Box Height: 10-15 feet

Wood Duck
Place in forested wetlands or near marshes, swamps, and beaver ponds; place boxes in deciduous trees (ones that lose their leaves seasonally) 30-100 feet from the nearest water and space boxes 600 feet apart. Add 3" of wood shavings.
Box Height: 6-30 feet

American Kestrel
Place in pastures, fields, meadows, or orchards with mowed or grazed vegetation; boxes may be placed on lone trees in fields, on trees along edges of woodlots, and on farm buildings.
Box Height: 10-30 feet

Eastern Screech Owl
Mount on tree in woodland clearings, forest edges, or wooded stream edges, preferably under a tree limb. Entrance hole should face north. Add 2"-3" of wood shavings.
Box Height: 10-30 feet

Western Screech Owl
Mount in lower elevations, forests, parks, woodland clearings, forest edges, deserts, or wooded stream edges, under a tree limb. Entrance hole should face north. Add 2"-3" of wood shavings.
Box Height: 10-30 feet

Great Crested Flycatcher
Mount on pole or post at forest edges, woodlots, orchards, or parks facing open area.
Box Height: 3-20 feet

Ash-throated Flycatcher
Place in chaparral or mesquite thickets, dry plains spotted with trees, or in cacti in deserts. Boxes can also be placed in open deciduous woodlands with a river or stream nearby.
Box Height: 3-20 feet

Northern Flicker
Mount on pole or tree in pastures, groves, woodlots, orchards, fields, meadows, woodland clearings, forest edges, or along fence rows bordering crop fields. Fill box completely with wood chips or shavings. Entrance hole should face southeast.
Box Height: 6-30 feet

Tree Swallow
Mount on a pole or post in an open field near water, in expansive open areas, marshes, meadows, or wooded swamps near a tree or fence at least 30 feet apart. Entrance hole should face east.
Box Height: 5-15 feet

Violet-green Swallow
Mount in open or spacious deciduous or mixed deciduous forests, wooded canyons, or edges of dense forest.
Box Height: 9-15 feet

Tufted Titmouse
Place in deciduous forest, woodland clearings, forest edges, woodlots, near river or stream; spaced one box per 8 acres. Hole should face away from prevailing wind.
Box Height: 5-15 feet

Black-capped Chickadee
Mount at forest edges, woodlots, and yards with well-established hardwood trees, or meadows in area that receives 40-60% sunlight. Space one box per 10 acres. Hole should face away from prevailing wind; 1" shavings can be placed in box.
Box Height: 5-15 feet

Carolina Chickadee
Mount at forest edges, woodlots, and yards with well-established hardwood trees, or meadows in areas that receives 40-60% sunlight. Hole should face away from prevailing wind; 1" shavings can be placed in box.
Box Height: 5-15 feet

Mountain Chickadee
Mount at dense forest edges or woodland clearings; hole should face away from prevailing wind; 1" shavings can be placed in box.
Box Height: 5-15 feet

Chestnut-backed Chickadee
Place in forests, forest edges, woodlands, thickets, or burned areas, near a water source such as a stream. Hole should face away from prevailing wind; 1" shavings can be placed in box.
Box Height: 5-15 feet

White-breasted Nuthatch
Place at mature forests, woodlots, near open areas, forest edges, or orchards, and near water. Hole should face away from prevailing wind; 1" shavings can be placed in box.
Box Height: 5-20 feet

Red-breasted Nuthatch
Place in forests, shrub lands, swamps, farmlands, and suburban yards. Hole should face away from prevailing wind; 1" shavings can be placed in box.
Box Height: 5-15 feet

Brown-headed Nuthatch
Place in open areas of pine-hardwood forests, clearings scattered with dead trees, forest edges, burned areas, or cypress swamps.
Box Height: 5-20 feet

House Wren
Adapts to a variety of habitats; place in farmland, open forests, forest edges, shrub lands, suburban yards and gardens, or parks, near trees or tall shrubs.
Box Height: 5-10 feet

Carolina Wren
Mount in forests with thick underbrush, forest edges, woodland clearings, shrub lands, suburban yards and gardens, or parks, near trees or tall shrubs.
Box Height: 5-10 feet

Prothonotary Warbler
Place box over or very close to water in lowland hardwood forests subject to flooding, stagnant water, swamps, ponds, marshes, streams, or flooded river valleys.
Box Height: 2-12 feet

Hooded Merganser
Prefers quiet, shallow, clear water pools surrounded by or near the edge of woods with deciduous trees that lose their leaves seasonally. Place near small forest pools, ponds, swamps. Add 3" of wood shavings.
Box Height: 6-25 feet

Final Thoughts

Expand your living space by hanging an **Outdoor Birdhouse** in a picture-perfect viewing spot. Take a moment each day to observe your creation from a deck chair or a window. Relax as you enjoy the magic of nature unfolding. Watch as birds explore a new nesting home possibility — the one you made! Cheer on the lucky ones as they transport their furnishings, one twig at a time. Welcome your new neighbors with seed and water and watch your family grow. While enjoying the new hustle and bustle in your yard, you may find yourself dreaming up your next birdhouse beauty!

For **Indoor Birdhouse Decorations** envision the final design before you begin. This unfinished birdhouse reminded me of the candy cottage Hansel and Gretel discovered. Remembering the enduring fairy tale inspired me to recreate this symbol of courage and love. During the house prep I left many of the wood splinters resembling candy crystals hanging from the roof and windows. I searched for and found candy themed pins, bracelets, necklaces and earrings before choosing the paint and coordinating colors.

Go ahead — sign your artwork! After all, you created an original!

About the Author

Holly DiBella-McCarthy resides in Connecticut with her husband Kevin. She is the proud mother of 3 grown children and enjoys vacationing with her family. A professional educator, Holly has dedicated her career to children with special education needs and is currently the director of special education for a public school district.

Share Your Photo!

Visit www.birdhousebeauties.com or birdhousebeautiesbyholly@gmail.com
and share your best birdhouse beauty!

www.ingramcontent.com/pod-product-compliance
Lightning Source LLC
Chambersburg PA
CBHW040026050426
42453CB00002B/22